GROWING UP IN WORLD WAR TWO
FOOD

Catherine Burch

W

FRANKLIN WATTS
LONDON•SYDNEY

First published in 2005
by Franklin Watts
96 Leonard Street, London
EC2A 4XD

Franklin Watts Australia
Level 17/207 Kent Street
Sydney, NSW 2000

© 2005 Franklin Watts

Produced for Franklin Watts by
White-Thomson Publishing Ltd,
Bridgewater Business Centre, 210 High Street,
Lewes, East Sussex, BN7 2NH

Consultant: Andrew Spooner, military historian
Design: Bernard Higton Design
The Publisher would like to thank Hulton Archive /
Getty Images for supplying all the photographs. Thanks
to the Wartime Memories Project for permission to
include quotations from its website.

A CIP catalogue record for this book is available from
the British Library.

ISBN 0 7496 6195 X

Printed in China.

CONTENTS

War begins 4

Rationing 6

Shopping 8

Dig for victory 10

Women's Land Army 12

On the farm 14

Pigs and poultry 16

Potatoes and bread 18

Ration-free meals 20

Wild food 22

Healthy times 24

New tastes 26

Treats 28

Glossary 30

Further information 31

Index 32

Words in the glossary are in **bold** the first time they appear.

Read all about it! 1939
A newspaper seller announces the **outbreak of war**. Britain and France declared war on Germany after it invaded Poland. Their governments decided they had given Adolf Hitler, Germany's leader, enough warnings.

NEWS OF THE WORLD
WAR DECLARED OFFICIAL

WAR BEGINS

World War Two began when Nazi Germany invaded Poland on 1 September 1939. Britain and France declared war against Germany on 3 September.

At the start of the war British farmers produced enough food for about one in three people in the country. The rest was **imported** from other parts of the world. As soon as the war began, German **U-boats** attacked and sank ships carrying food and supplies to Britain. British farmers had to grow more so that everyone in the country had enough to eat.

Careless words, 1940
This poster shows a British ship sinking. It warns people not to share secrets in case German spies heard them, and passed information to the enemy.

A FEW CARELESS WORDS MAY END IN THIS—
Many lives were lost in the last war through careless talk
Be on your guard! Don't discuss movements of ships or troops

RATIONING

Rationing was introduced in January 1940 to ensure that the food available was shared out fairly.

At first, sugar, butter, bacon and ham were rationed. You were allowed to buy only a small amount of these foods each week. Later in the war other foods – such as all meat, cheese, eggs, tea, sweets and chocolate – were also rationed. Everyone had a ration book that showed how much you could buy. Some non-food items also had to be rationed. These included petrol and clothing.

Three ration books, 1943
This picture shows ration books for meat, cooking fats and other foods. If you lost your ration book, you could not buy what you wanted until you got a new one from the Ministry of Food.

By the book, 1943
A woman uses her ration book to buy food at a **grocer's shop**. At some shops, such as the butcher's, you had to register (put your name on a list) to be able to buy food there.

That's your lot
A typical family's weekly rations. People could also eat food that wasn't rationed, but there were shortages of many things as the war went on.

Jam

Sugar

Tea

Bacon

Dried eggs

Cheese

Meat

Lard

Margarine

Butter

SHOPPING

In the 1940s not many homes had refrigerators. As a result, fresh food spoiled quickly.

People did not shop for food in big supermarkets, like we do today. They went shopping every day, going to separate baker's, butcher's, grocer's and **greengrocer's shops**. Wartime shortages meant that you had to take your own bags when you went shopping because there was very little paper. You even had to take your own paper to the chip shop to wrap up fish and chips.

A rare sight, 1941
A man sells bananas on a London street. Bananas were imported, and therefore very **scarce** during the war. Many children grew up not knowing what a banana tasted like.

Please join the queue, 1941
People queue up at a greengrocer's to buy oranges from a special delivery. Shortages meant that people got used to queuing for things.

I REMEMBER ....
'Cookery lessons were funny, we learned to make do with what was available. We made fish cakes with mashed potatoes, ground rice, parsley and some kind of fish sauce to give them flavour.'
•••••••••••••••••••••••••••• (Kath, from *The World War Two Memories Project*)

DIG FOR VICTORY

The British government asked farmers to plough up as much land as they could to grow more food for the country.

It also encouraged people to grow vegetables in their gardens. Families dug up their lawns and planted carrots and potatoes. They saw this as their way of helping to win the war. Posters appeared in towns saying: 'Dig for Victory'. Public parks, railway embankments and bomb sites were made into **allotments** for growing vegetables.

Pick your own, 1941
Boys return from tending vegetables in their school's allotment. Some schools grew vegetables in their grounds and then served them up with school dinners.

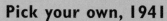

Tomato toil, 1942
Growing your own tomatoes was a popular thing to do. As the war went on, more foods – such as rice, tinned fruit and tomatoes – became scarce.

A moat point, 1940
People dug for victory in many surprising places. This is the **moat** of the Tower of London.

WOMEN'S LAND ARMY

Farmers could produce more food by growing fields of crops rather than by keeping animals. Many herds of cows were killed to make more fields available.

However, farmers did not have enough workers to help harvest crops because so many young men had gone away to fight. So, thousands of young women **volunteered** to join the **Women's Land Army**. They were known as 'Land Girls' and made a big contribution to Britain's war effort.

Fleecy four, 1941
Four 'Land Girls' shear sheep in London's Hyde Park. Land Girls were paid very little but worked extremely hard. They were allowed just seven days' holiday a year.

'Lend a hand on the land!' 1942
Young women from the Women's Land Army use a hay-baling machine on a farm. They wore a uniform of short-sleeved shirts and breeches. or dungarees. When they were not working they wore brown felt hats and khaki overcoats.

ON THE FARM

The German air force bombed many British towns and cities. Thousands of children were evacuated to safer parts of the country. Many went to live on farms.

Evacuees living on farms had to help with the chores; some had to work very hard. However, people generally had more to eat in the country because it was easier to grow vegetables, keep chickens and gather wild fruit.

Cuddly lambs, 1940
Some evacuees were very homesick, but others loved living in the countryside. This picture shows three girls from London having a wonderful time cuddling a farmer's lambs.

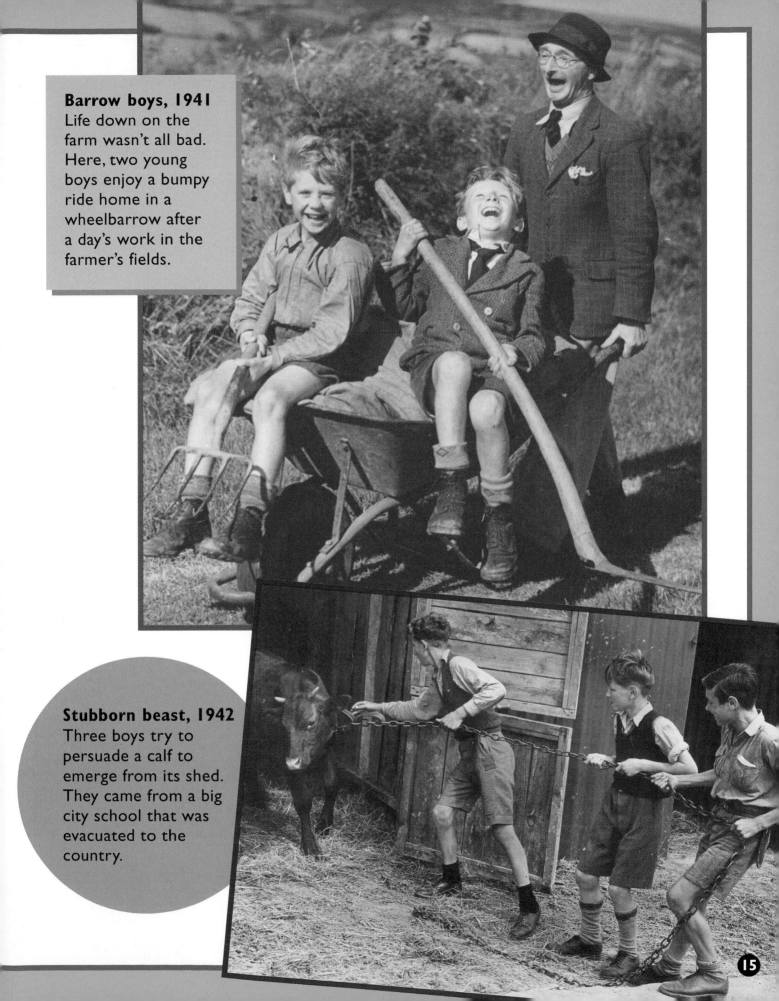

Barrow boys, 1941
Life down on the farm wasn't all bad. Here, two young boys enjoy a bumpy ride home in a wheelbarrow after a day's work in the farmer's fields.

Stubborn beast, 1942
Three boys try to persuade a calf to emerge from its shed. They came from a big city school that was evacuated to the country.

PIGS AND POULTRY

Meat and eggs were rationed, so many people started to keep their own pigs and chickens.

Many people joined Pig Clubs. They saved kitchen waste, such as dry bread and vegetable peelings, to feed pigs. When the animals were slaughtered (killed), members shared the meat. This rhyme from a Ministry of Food advert told people that keeping pigs was a way of helping to fight the war:

*'Because of the **pail**, the scraps were saved,*
Because of the scraps, the pigs were saved,
Because of the pigs, the rations were saved,
Because of the rations, the ships were saved,
Because of the ships, the island was saved,
Because of the island, the Empire was saved,
And all because of the housewife's pail.'

Poultry proud, 1940
A boy shows off a fine goose. His school in Harrogate started a 'pig and poultry' club. Many schools changed their timetables to fit in activities like pig keeping and vegetable growing.

Porkers on parade, 1941
Keeping pigs became quite fashionable.
Groups of workers, like these firemen,
got together to raise pigs.

WYSE PIG CLUB

POTATOES AND BREAD

British farmers could not grow enough wheat to make bread for everyone. So the government encouraged people to eat potatoes instead of bread.

A cartoon character called 'Potato Pete' was invented. He encouraged people to fill themselves up with potatoes. A new loaf of bread, called the National Wheatmeal Loaf, was introduced in 1942. This was made from whole wheat to help people maintain good health. However, Britons weren't used to eating brown bread and it was very unpopular.

Pick of the crop, 1943
Evacuees from a school in Essex help a local farmer to harvest the potato crop.

Use your loaf, 1942
A baker shows people
how to make the new
National Wheatmeal
Loaf. Bread was so
precious that you could
be fined for wasting it —
even for feeding it to
the birds!

Balls of flour, 1944
These potatoes were
labelled 'Balls of Flour'
to encourage people to
believe that potatoes
were as tasty
as bread. Potatoes
could be grown easily.

RATION-FREE MEALS

One way to obtain a meal 'off the ration' was to eat out at a restaurant. Take-away fish and chips were not rationed either.

More people started to eat at restaurants during the war. They also ate away from home in factory **canteens**, and in schools that started to provide school dinners. A chain of cafés called the 'New British Restaurants' was set up to help people whose homes or work canteens had been bombed during the **Blitz**. They served good, cheap food.

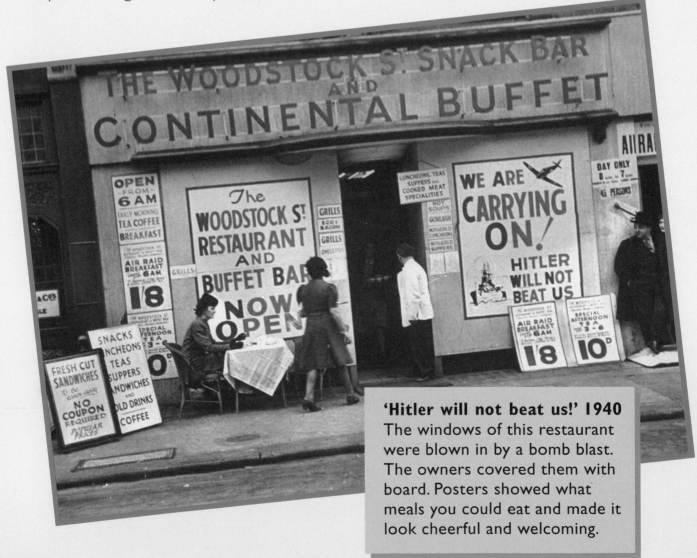

'Hitler will not beat us!' 1940
The windows of this restaurant were blown in by a bomb blast. The owners covered them with board. Posters showed what meals you could eat and made it look cheerful and welcoming.

Canteen queue, 1942
Many schools started serving school dinners for the first time during the war. For some children, this was the best meal of the day. One in three children ate a meal at school by the end of the war in 1945.

I REMEMBER ....

'One day I was sent to get fish and chips. You had to take your own newspaper to wrap them in, but my Mum didn't have any. The shop could only let me have one sheet of paper to wrap the fish and chips in, so the parcel was really hot and burned my hands. On the way home the grease made the paper go soggy and fall apart, and I began to drop the chips. When I got home my coat was covered in grease and I had dropped a lot of our meal. Luckily my Mum was only cross with the shopkeeper.'

(Girl, Biggleswade)

WILD FOOD

Rationed food could be boring and portions were usually too small. As a result, people often went hungry. Hunting or gathering wild food helped.

People hunted rabbits and pigeons. They also picked blackberries, mushrooms, nuts, rosehips and other things that grew wild in hedgerows and fields to make meals more interesting. Families and groups of Brownies and Cubs went out into the country to pick wild fruit to make into jam.

Bunny hunter, 1941
A man reaches down a hole to try and catch a rabbit. Rabbits were a good free source of meat. More people ate rabbit in the 1940s than we do today.

Jammy job, 1943
Women and children in Kent pick blackberries to sell to jam factories. In the summer, people could get extra sugar rations for making jam.

I REMEMBER...........
'Much of my childhood seemed to be spent foraging the countryside. We picked wild strawberries, raspberries and blackberries, all for jam, or to eat as a treat with milk.'

●●●●●●●●●●●●●●●●●●●●● (Girl, Lewes)

HEALTHY TIMES

Wartime rationing actually improved people's health. For the first time everyone had enough basic, healthy food.

People were forced to eat less fatty foods, such as butter, **lard**, cheese and meat, because they were in short supply. Everyone had to eat more vegetables and fruit. The government realised that people needed to be well fed so they could work harder and longer hours. That way, Britain was more likely to win the war.

Four pints, please, 1941
Most people had their milk delivered to their doorstep during the war. Milk was important in a healthy diet, especially for children and pregnant women.

Harvest of health, 1940
The 'Dig for Victory' campaign led many people to grow their own fruit and vegetables. The extra vegetables people ate during the war were very good for their health.

NEW TASTES

The war was a time when people tried all sorts of new things to eat.

Some foods, such as **dried eggs,** were unpopular, but others were big hits. To make use of what food was available, many odd recipes – such as carrot marmalade – were invented. As a result of the **Lend-Lease Agreement** in 1941, the USA began to send more food to Britain. British shops started to sell tins of **Spam** (chopped pork and ham) and corned beef – people loved it!

Over here, 1942
US soldiers and airmen began to arrive in Britain in 1942. They were very popular with children because they gave away sweets and chewing gum.

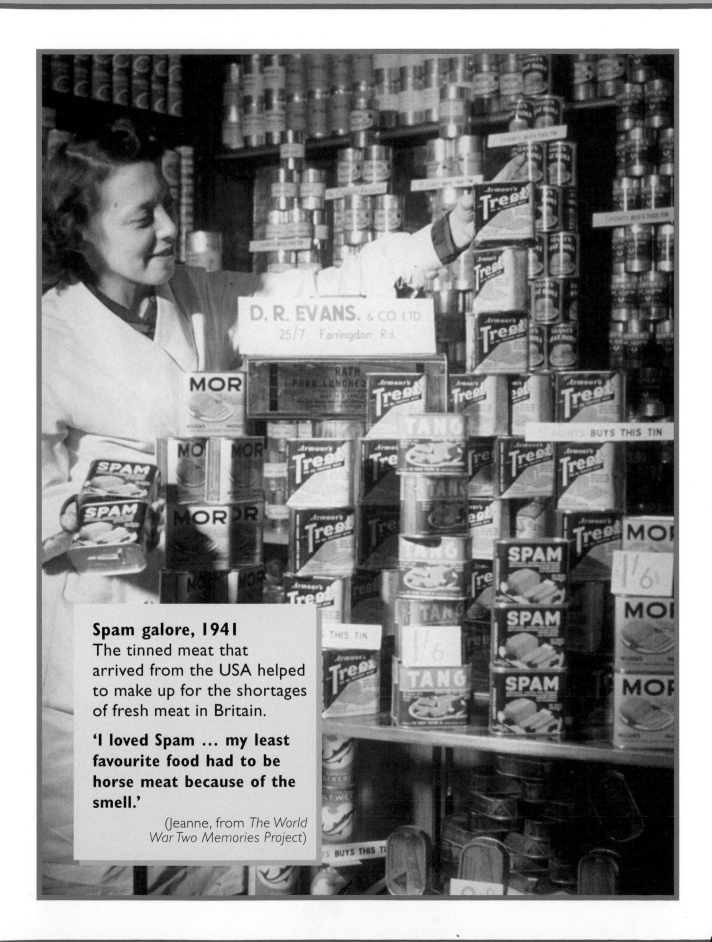

Spam galore, 1941
The tinned meat that arrived from the USA helped to make up for the shortages of fresh meat in Britain.

'I loved Spam ... my least favourite food had to be horse meat because of the smell.'

(Jeanne, from *The World War Two Memories Project*)

TREATS

Sweets and sugar were rationed because sugar had to be imported. Eggs, butter and flour were also in short supply so it wasn't easy to make treats, such as cakes.

People had to save up their rations if they wanted to have a party, and the guests usually had to bring food as well. Ice cream became an impossible **luxury** during the war, as there wasn't enough milk to make it.

I REMEMBER..........

'I remember one day an air raid came over and a bomb dropped nearby, shattering all the windows in the street. The sweet shop had just had a delivery of sweets, and they were blown out with the glass all over the road, not fit to eat. It seemed a terrible waste to me.'

●●●●●●●●●● (Girl, Lewes)

Juicy treat, 1941
Young boys at a nursery school enjoy a great treat — half an orange each!

Carrot lollies, 1941
For most children (and many grown ups) the sweets ration was never enough. Here, three children eat big carrots on sticks for a snack.

What, no jelly? 1945
The end of the war in Europe came when Germany surrendered (gave up) on 7 May 1945. The government declared 8 May VE (Victory in Europe) Day, and there were street parties all over Britain. However, food rationing continued until 1954.

GLOSSARY

Air raid a sudden attack from the air, such as the nightly attacks on Britain by German planes during the Blitz

Allies the countries fighting against Germany and Japan. The main Allies were Britain and its empire, France, USA and the USSR.

Allotment an area of land in a village or town that you can pay rent to use for growing things, such as fruit and vegetables

Blitz the heavy bombing of Britain's towns, factories and railways by the German air force in the early war years

Canteen a café where food is served to people at schools and factories or other large workplaces

Dried eggs eggs that were dried to a powder. Dried eggs were imported from the USA. A packet of dried egg took up much less space on a ship than a dozen fresh eggs.

Evacuate send away for safety. Children and mothers with babies that lived in the most dangerous areas were sent to live somewhere safer.

Evacuee someone who was evacuated

Greengrocer's shop a shop selling fruit and vegetables

Grocer's shop a shop selling food and other household supplies, such as sugar, cereal, tea, tinned food and soap. Grocer's shops have mostly been replaced by supermarkets.

Imported bought in from another country to sell in your own country

Lard cooking fat that comes in a solid block like butter

Lend-Lease Agreement an agreement whereby the USA gave food and equipment to Britain as a loan, which did not have to be paid back until after the war

Luxury something expensive, comfortable, a treat

Moat a ditch around a castle, usually filled with water, to keep out attackers

Outbreak of war the opening, or beginning of a war

Pail bucket

Rationing allowing an equal share to everyone. Food, petrol and clothing were all rationed during World War Two.

Scarce not enough available, or in short supply

Spam a mixture of ready-to-eat pork and ham, in a tin

U-boat German submarine

Volunteer offer to do something

Women's Land Army women could volunteer join the Women's Land Army. They were sent all around the country to help on farms, driving tractors, planting potatoes and looking after animals.

FURTHER INFORMATION

Books

Butterfield, Moira, *Going to War in World War Two* (Franklin Watts, 2001)

Cooper, Alison, *Rationing* (Hodder Wayland, 2003)

Deary, Terry, *Horrible History, The Woeful Second World War* (Hippo, 1999)

Hamley, Dennis, *The Second World War* (Franklin Watts, 2004)

Masters, Anthony, *World War II Stories* (Franklin Watts, 2004)

Parsons, Martin, *Britain at War: Rationing* (Wayland, 1999)

Reynoldson, Fiona, *The Past in Pictures: The Home Front* (Wayland, 1999)

Reynoldson, Fiona, *What Families Were Like: The Second World War* (Hodder Wayland, 2002)

Ross, Stewart, *Rationing* (Evans, 2002)

Websites

Fun interactive BBC site in which you can pretend to go shopping in wartime Britain, read letters from evacuees and hear the sound of an air raid warning:
http://www.bbc.co.uk/history/ww2children//index.shtml

Home Sweet Home Front site containing useful information, and interesting photos and posters on various key topics: rationing, dig for victory, land girls, evacuees, squander:
http://www.homesweethomefront.co.uk/templates/hshf_frameset_tem.htm

The Second World War Experience Centre site, with descriptions of aspects of life on the home front, and memories from those who experienced it:
http://www.war-experience.org/history/keyaspects/home-british/

The World War Two Memories Project. An interactive site containing questions to and answers from people who lived through World War Two:
http://www.wartimememories.co.uk/questions.html

Note to parents and teachers

Every effort has been made by the Publishers to ensure that these websites are suitable for children, that they are of the highest educational value, and that they contain no inappropriate or offensive material. However, because of the nature of the Internet, it is impossible to guarantee that the contents of these sites will not be altered. We strongly advise that Internet access is supervised by a responsible adult.

INDEX

allotments 10
animals (farm) 12, 13, 14, 15, 16, 17

bakers' shops 8
bananas 8
berries 22, 23
bombing 20, 28
bread 18, 19
butchers' shops 7, 8
butter 6, 24, 28

cheese 6, 24
chickens 14, 16
cookery lessons 9, 19

'Dig for Victory' 10, 25

eggs 6, 26, 28
evacuees 14, 15, 18

farmers 5, 10, 12, 14, 18
fish and chips 8, 20, 21
fruit 8, 9, 14, 22, 23, 24, 25, 28

greengrocers' shops 8
grocers' shops 7, 8

imports 5, 28

jam 22, 23

Land Girls 12

meat 6, 22, 24, 26, 27
milk 24
Ministry of Food 6

parties 28, 29
Pig Clubs 16, 17
Potato Pete 18
potatoes 18, 19

queues 9

rabbits 22
ration books 6, 7
rationing 6, 7, 24
rations (weekly) 7, 23, 28
recipes 26
restaurants 20

schools 10, 16, 20, 21
ships 5
shopping 7, 8, 9
shopping bags 8
sugar 6, 23, 28
sweets 6, 26, 28, 29

U-boats 5
USA 26, 27

vegetables 10, 11, 14, 16, 24, 25

war, outbreak of 4, 5
Women's Land Army 12, 13